WS

Black Widow Spider

Monica Harris

www.heinemann.co.uk
Visit our website to find out more information about Heinemann Library books.

To order:
 Phone 44 (0) 1865 888066
Send a fax to 44 (0) 1865 314091
Visit the Heinemann Bookshop at www.heinemann.co.uk to browse our catalogue and order online.

First published in Great Britain by Heinemann Library, Halley Court, Jordan Hill, Oxford OX2 8EJ, part of Harcourt Education Ltd. Heinemann is a registered trademark of Harcourt Education Ltd.

Editorial: Barbara Katz, Kathy Peltan
Designed by Ginkgo Creative, Inc.
Printed and bound in the United States by Lake Book Manufacturing, Inc.
Picture research by Scott Braut
Production: John Nelson, Viv Hichens

ISBN 0 431 01724 7
07 06 05 04 03
10 9 8 7 6 5 4 3 2 1

British Library Cataloguing in Publication Data
Harris, Monica
  Black widow spider. - (Bug books)
  1.Black widow spider - Juvenile literature
  1.Title
  595.4'4
A full catalogue record for this book is available from the British Library.

Acknowledgments
The author and publishers are grateful to the following for permission to reproduce copyright material: pp. 4, 7 Dr. James L. Castner; p. 5 E. R. Degginger/Photo Researchers, Inc.; pp. 6, 16, 23 James C. Cokendolpher; p. 8 Tom McHugh/Photo Researchers, Inc.; pp. 9, 12 J. H. Robinson/Photo Researchers, Inc.; p. 10 Ann & Rob Simpson; p. 11 David T. Roberts/Nature's Images/Photo Researchers, Inc.; pp. 13, 14, 15, 24 Daniel Heuclin/NHPA; p. 17 Mark Cassino; p. 18 Robert Brenner/PhotoEdit; p. 19 Index Stock Imagery, Inc.; p. 20 Dane S. Johnson/Visuals Unlimited; pp. 21, 25, 28 James H. Robinson; p. 22 Museum of Science Boston; p. 26 David A. Northcott/Corbis; p. 27 Visuals Unlimited; p. 29 Doug Sokell/Visuals Unlimited.

Illustration, p. 30, by Will Hobbs.

Cover photograph by Scott Camazine/Oxford Scientific Films.

Special thanks to Dr. William Shear, Department of Biology, Hampden-Sydney College, Virginia, USA for his review of this book.

Any words in the text in bold, **like this**, are explained in the Glossary.

Contents

What are black widow spiders?

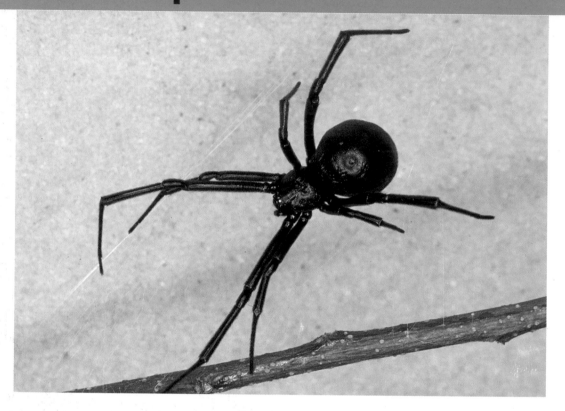

Black widows **spiders** are **arachnids**.
They have eight legs and eight eyes.
Black widows can be brown or black.

Black widows make **silk webs** to trap **insects**. Then they use special mouthparts to kill the insect. Black widow spiders are very **venomous**.

What do black widow spiders look like?

The black widow's body has two parts.
The head and chest are in the smaller
part, called the **cephalothorax**. The
larger part is the **abdomen**.

Black widows have red marks under their abdomens. The marks can be two small dots or two triangles connected at their points. **Males** also have red stripes on their sides.

How big are black widow spiders?

The **female** black widow's body is about the size of a pea. It has two front legs that are longer than its other legs.

The **male** has a much smaller body and longer legs than the female. His **abdomen** is shaped like an egg. The female's abdomen is round.

How are black widow spiders born?

Black widow **spiders mate** in the spring. Then the **female** makes a **silk egg sac**. The silk comes from her **spinnerets**. She lays from 250 to 750 eggs inside the egg sac.

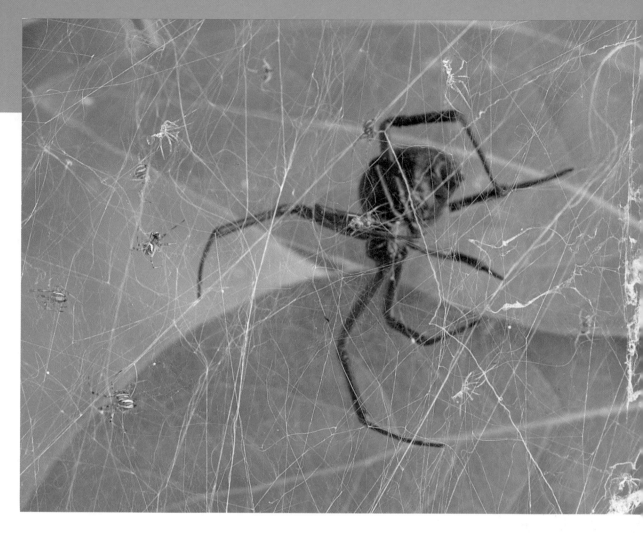

The eggs **hatch** after twenty days. The baby spiders are called **spiderlings**. They are tiny and white. Spiderlings stay in the **web** with their mother, but she does not take care of them.

How do black widow spiders grow?

As the **spiderlings** grow, their skin becomes too small. They **shed** their skin for a new and bigger one. This is called **moulting**.

When the spiderlings are old enough, they spin a thread of **silk**. The wind catches the thread. The spiderlings float away to a new home. They move like a balloon in the wind.

What do black widow spiders eat?

Black widow **spiders** eat **insects** such as crickets and beetles. They make a **web** of sticky **silk**. Insects get stuck in the web.

Black widows use their **fangs** to put **venom** into insects. The venom stops them from moving. Then, the spiders suck the juices from the insect's body.

15

Which animals attack black widow spiders?

Wasps and other **spiders**, like this pirate spider, eat black widows. Black widows try to run away. Sometimes they lift their front legs in the air to scare the enemy away.

This wasp may sting a black widow spider and put it into a nest with her eggs. The wasp **larvae** will eat the spider when they **hatch**.

Where do black widow spiders live?

Black widows live in warm places. They build their **webs** away from people. A black widow **spider** might make a home in a pile of wood.

Black widows also live in sheds, outbuildings, rubbish piles or hollow trees. **Females** live in dark places. They move around at night.

How long do black widow spiders live?

Female black widows live longer than **males**. They usually live about eighteen months. Males live about seven months.

Some baby black widows live for only a few days. **Spiderlings** are very hungry when they **hatch**. Sometimes they eat each other. This is called **cannibalism**.

How do black widow spiders move?

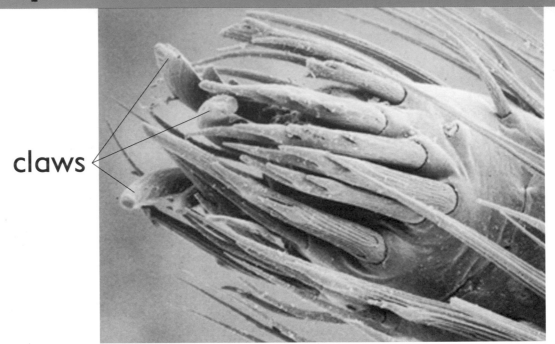

claws

Spiders use their eight legs to walk. Three small claws at the end of each leg help them to hang on to things. They can even walk up walls.

Females hang upside down in their **webs**. They only leave when in danger. **Males** do not spin webs. When they leave their **burrow**, they walk on the ground to find food.

What do black widow spiders do?

The **female** black widow may eat the **male** after they **mate**. But they usually just eat lots of **insects**. This **protects** gardens because insects eat lots of plants.

Each female makes from four to nine **egg sacs** in the summer. There are thousands of eggs. But only a few **spiderlings** will live to become adults.

How are black widow spiders special?

The black widow is one of the most **venomous spiders**. Only the **females** have **venom**. One drop is more poisonous than a drop of rattlesnake venom!

These spiders are very shy. They usually do not bite humans. Most bites happen when people walk into a black widow's **web** by mistake.

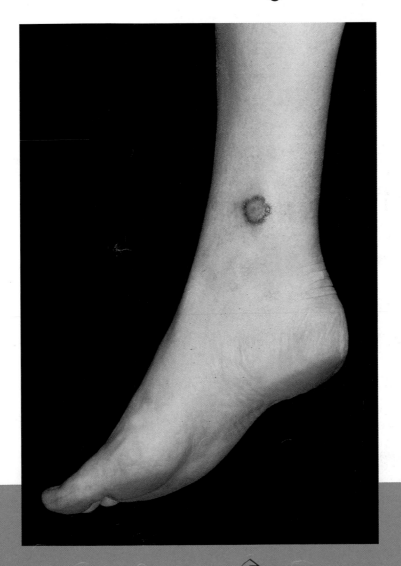

Thinking about black widow spiders

Which of these black widow **spiders** is the **male**? Which is the **female**? How can you tell?

This female black widow has trapped a large **insect** in her **web**. She will use her **fangs** to bite it. What do her fangs put into the insect?

Black widow spider map

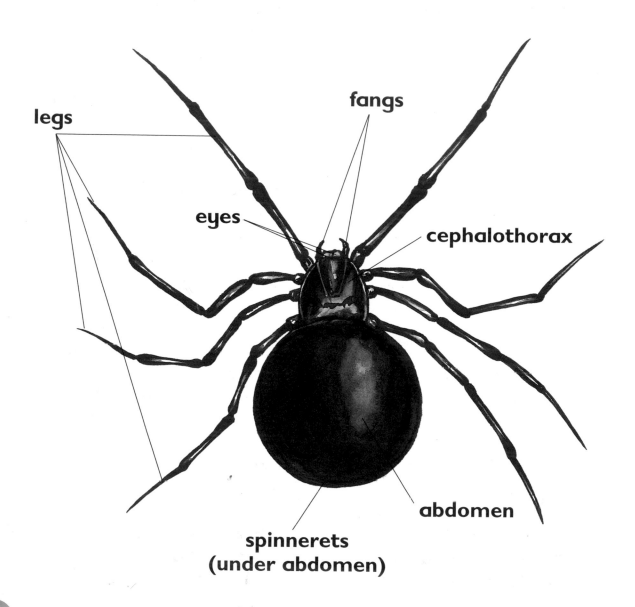

legs

fangs

eyes

cephalothorax

abdomen

spinnerets
(under abdomen)

Glossary

abdomen stomach area of an animal

arachnids group of animals that includes spiders, ticks and scorpions. They have eight legs and two body parts.

burrow animal's home, usually in the ground

cannibalism when an animal eats one of its own kind

cephalothorax (you say sef-uh-luh-thor-ax), body part that is both the head and chest

egg sac bag that holds eggs

fang special mouthpart with tube for venom

female girl, mother

hatch to be born from an egg

insect animal with six legs and three body parts

larvae young of an animal that looks like a worm

male boy, father

mate when a male and a female come together to make babies

moult get rid of skin that is too small

prey animal eaten by other animals

protect keep safe

shed fall off or lose

silk thin, shiny thread

spider animal with eight legs and two body parts. Most spiders make webs.

spiderling baby spider

spinnerets body parts that makes silk

venom poison used when biting to stop an insect from moving

venomous uses poison venom to kill animal or make it very sick

web threads of silk connected together to make a net

Index